NOW HEAR THIS

NOW HEAR THIS

Harper soars with her magic ears

VALLI GIDEONS AND HARPER GIDEONS

gatekeeper press

Columbus, Ohio

Now Hear This: Harper soars with her magic ears

Published by Gatekeeper Press
2167 Stringtown Rd, Suite 109
Columbus, OH 43123-2989
www.GatekeeperPress.com

The cover design, interior formatting, typesetting, and editorial work for this book are entirely the product of the author. Gatekeeper Press did not participate in and is not responsible for any aspect of these elements.

ISBN (hardcover): 9781642379020
ISBN (paperback): 9781642379037
eISBN: 9781642379044

This book is dedicated to my children, Battle and Harper.
Being their advocate has been the greatest honor of my life. What I didn't know
all those years ago when we began this hearing loss journey is what being their
momma would teach me about strength, resiliency, and love. Because of them,
I have discovered the deepest kind of love, the type of love you can only imagine
in your dreams. I can't wait to continue watching them soar!
—Valli Gideons

This is dedicated to the ones who are not afraid to step out of their comfort
zones and be themselves. And, to those who are ready to soar but still need to
find their wings!
—Harper Gideons

Acknowledgements

The authors of this book acknowledge the following persons who were instrumental in the creation of this book.

Veni Fields – I appreciate your friendship and guidance—dating back to the college course: Journalism 101. Your expert editing skills and magical gift of writing have made this project so meaningful.

Adrienne Hedger – We can't thank you enough for lending your guidance and gift of storytelling to this project. You are talented beyond measure.

Nancy "Spoons" Bsharah and Belinda Leung – My two closest friends, dating all the way back to elementary school, encouraged me not only to start writing again after a long hiatus but also to share our hearing loss journey. You have been by my side cheering for me every step of the way.

Rian Otto – A fantastic teacher, you also have a unique gift of capturing the essence of the person through the lens of a camera. Thank you for lending your exceptional photography talents for this project and truly "seeing" Harper and Battle.

Mom (aka "Grandma Sharry") – Thank you for always believing in us and lending your support in so many ways to help this book come to fruition. You have always known our kids would soar and have been one of their greatest cheerleaders.

Chris Gideons (aka "Dad") – Last, but certainly not least, so much gratitude for this guy. Thank you for being our family's rock and supporting our passions and dreams. There is no one we would rather navigate life with than you!

There are so many people in our lives who have made an impact. We feel incredibly grateful. To those along the way who have believed in our kids and encouraged them to soar: Thank you! Family, friends, teachers, therapists, coaches, specialists, and the like— we profoundly appreciate your love and support.

I came into the world healthy and with gusto. "She's perfectly petite!" the doctor said. My mom and dad quickly nicknamed me "The Bean."

So there I was... a happy little Bean. Only my tiny ears didn't work like other kids'. My mom and dad had this weird gene thing that caused a part of the inside of my ear to be enlarged—by the size of a hair.

The size of a hair isn't much, you might think. But when it comes to that part of the ear, believe me, it matters.

That little difference means I have a hearing loss. Some people like to call it "hard of hearing" or deaf. You can think of it kind of like people who wear glasses to improve their eyesight. I need a hearing device to help me hear. Except, hearing aids can only make the things you can hear louder, where glasses can help some people see crystal clear. See what I mean? Kind of the same but a little bit different.

My hearing loss meant many trips to doctors. You know how certain things are just a regular part of life for babies? Like eating, sleeping, and pooping? Well, visiting doctors became a regular part of mine.

One doctor was called an ENT. That's short for Ear, Nose, and Throat. He never did look at my nose or throat, he just focused on my ears. A LOT. That might seem scary, but my mom and dad were experts by the time I was born because here's something that is wild: Can you believe my big brother, Battle, was also born with hearing loss? I am guessing by the time I came along, my parents knew tons about ears.

Having hearing loss meant we also made lots of visits to an audiologist, who is a super smart kind of doctor trained in all things hearing. She was the one who fitted me for my first pair of hearing aids. She put gooey stuff in my ear to

make ear molds that went with my hearing aids, and I even got to choose the colors. I picked my favorite combination: blue ear molds and silver hearing aids.

One thing I realized right away: Hearing aids make everything louder. Mine were digital and programmed specifically for me so I could hear better.

I liked my hearing aids, but I was a little kid learning "fine motor skills" (that's when you learn to use your fingers and hands). And guess what. I loved to pull out my hearing aids!

My mom and dad put them right back in and sang a "magic ear" song: "Magic ears, magic ears…listening is so much fun with magic ears!"

I would smile, then pull them right back out. In, out, in, out. What a fun game! I bet it drove my parents a little crazy.

When I was almost two years old, I had surgery to get something called a cochlear implant. Get ready, because this is cool: This implant was a super-duper amazing piece of technology that allowed me to hear things, similar to other boys and girls. Something else that is amazing is that the cochlear implant bypassed the part of my ear that didn't work, so that enlarged part inside of my ear didn't matter anymore.

Even though the idea of having surgery might seem kind of scary, it really wasn't. My parents held my hand and told me it would be over in the blink of an eye. And, boy, were they right. It was like I just fell asleep and the next thing I knew, my mom and dad were back by my side, and the surgery was all done. That's the cool thing about the anesthesia, which is the sleeping medicine they give you during surgery. You pretty much don't feel or remember anything about the surgery. Also cool: You can't believe the amount of ice cream I enjoyed after the surgery. And gifts. And snuggles. And cartoons. I felt like a queen. The Queen Bean.

Once I recovered from surgery, it was time to turn the cochlear implant on. I was so excited to go to the audiologist! She hooked up my new magic ear (that's what we called it) to her computer and programmed it just for me.

I played listening games during our programming sessions and got rewards, like lollipops and stickers, for trying my best. I'm telling you, the first time my new implant was turned on, my eyes got wide as saucers. Before, the world sounded a little bit muffled, but after the implant was turned on, everything sounded so clear and awesome.

Did having an implant stop me from pulling it off sometimes? Of course not! I was a toddler. My mom says she would find it in the sandbox, stuck to the refrigerator, or even buried in my car seat. One time I tossed it right into the gorilla cage at the zoo. Sorry, Mom!

But, just like with my hearing aid, my mom and dad put it right back on and sang the magic ear song.

It didn't take me long to figure out that keeping my cochlear implant on was a good thing. Maybe it didn't belong in a gorilla cage after all.

It helped me hear amazing sounds like birds chirping, ocean waves crashing, my favorite songs, and even the rain. Who knew there were so many awesome sounds to enjoy!

People ask me what it's like to hear with a cochlear implant. I'm not sure what to say because it's the only way I have ever heard.

But I can tell you this: It really helps when people face me while they speak. It's also helpful if they don't cover their mouths. People might not realize this, but I lip-read to help make more sense of what's being said.

Oh, also, there's no need to shout. I just need people to speak clearly and one person at a time. If I ask someone to repeat something, I hope they don't say "never mind." That makes me feel left out and kind of cruddy. I just need to hear it again clearly.

Families choose different forms of communication. There are kids who use hearing aids, kids who have cochlear implants, kids who use sign language, kids who wear bone conductors, and a combination of some of these.

I wear a hearing aid on one side and a cochlear implant on the other. My brother has bilateral cochlear implants. That means he has one on each side. My friend from school, Sam, wears hearing aids and also uses sign language to communicate. Joel, who lives in my neighborhood, wears a bone conductor headband that allows him to hear through the vibrations of the bones in his face. Check this out: Even Beethoven, who was a famous composer and also hard of hearing, used bone conduction to listen to music by biting down on his composer's wand while he touched it to the piano as he played.

At school, I usually sit near the front of the classroom. My teachers wear a special microphone that sends sound right into my ear. How cool is that? But, once in a while, they forget to turn it off before they go to the restroom or teacher's lounge. Awkward!

You might think all this stuff with my ears was a problem. But now that I'm twelve, I realize I've never thought there was anything I couldn't do. Being born with hearing loss hasn't stopped me one bit.

When I was little, I started playing basketball and was pretty good, so I've stuck with it. Gyms can be loud, though,

which makes it harder to hear my coach and teammates. My teammates use hand signals that my coach and I made up to call out the plays, in case I can't hear them. It's like our own secret language!

I love playing sports for so many reasons. But one is to show other kids that even with a hearing loss you can still compete and do anything your hearing friends can do.

Off the court, I love to read and write. My mom says someday I might be a professional writer. I mostly read adventure books. I imagine someday I'll climb a mountain and travel to far off places.

The thing about hearing loss is there is no one-size-fits-all. No two people experience it the same way.

We are each as unique as a fingerprint.

Take my brother – he likes playing football and hanging out in a small group of friends. He's learning to play the guitar and speak Chinese. Then there's me – who doesn't shy away from the spotlight and even had a part in my school's play. I love to build things using power tools and to play with my dogs. I have a deaf friend, Poppy, who is an artist. Her brother, Naish, who also has hearing loss, loves to play video games. My friend, Ryland, who is hard of hearing, plays hockey and collects LEGOs.

The one thing we all have in common is that we want to be treated like any other kid. We want to be included and accepted.

My mom and dad have always helped me believe I can achieve anything I put my mind to. They call me determined and tenacious. I don't know about that. I do know I've

learned to skateboard, snow ski, play sports, and I'm a pretty good student.

The bar has been set pretty high for me. But I'm positive I'm going to rise above it.

My parents no longer sing the magic ear song because I love wearing my cochlear implant. Except when my big brother is being annoying... then I want to toss it (or better yet, him) into a gorilla cage.

This is just a small piece of my hearing journey. I want you to know, no matter how tiny you are when you enter this world, or if you're hard of hearing or born with something else that challenges you—

You can reach. Rise. And soar! Just like me.

"Baby Bean" wearing her first pair of hearing aids. This was right about the time her "fine-motor" skills began to really be perfected and the "Magic Ear Song" was created.

Always looking toward the stars, Harper was captured here imagining the awesome places she might soar to.

As a toddler, Harper blowing bubbles shortly after her cochlear implant was activated. She has always gravitated towards being outside in nature.

Hoop Dreams. This is Harper's first season of club basketball. She was fearless and affectionately became known as "The Fighter."

Always moving with unabashed gusto, little Harper enjoyed her time working on her balance and agility with some amazing help from friends at a local physical/occupational therapy center.

With big brother, Battle, by her side, both kids proudly wave their home state's flag.

Being a military kid is a unique experience. There are lots of separations due to deployments and moving a lot is common. Battle and Harper proudly stand next to their Daddy, who has been serving in the Marine Corps long before they were born.

Harper's first elementary school self-portrait that she included her cochlear implant and hearing aid. This made her Mom's heart sing. Self-acceptance is so amazing!

Always searching for the next mountain to climb, Harper learns to snow ski and it doesn't take her long to look for steeper and more challenging slopes to conquer.

Skateboarding is another way Harper has found she can soar. Pictured here with one of Harper's best friends, Amaya, the girls are always plotting the next thing to climb.

Lake life is the best life. Battle and Harper have discovered one of their happy places is being near the water (no matter how cold it might be)! Utilizing their Aqua Ear covers has made water sports so much fun.

We have met some pretty amazing deaf and hard of hearing friends. Some of them are pictured here. They were all invited by our favorite audiologist, Dr. Joan Hewitt, to speak on a panel for a college class that she teaches. Right to left/Front row: Poppy, Harper, Ryland, Colt. Right to left/Back row: Dr. Joan, Battle, Naish.

A family that skies together, stays together. Or something like that… Enjoying family activities makes life so much fun.

One of our favorite pastimes is spending time with our shelter dogs, Jelly & JJ. Having pets has shown us what unconditional love looks like.

Perhaps setting the bar high and believing the sky is the limit is in Battle's and Harper's blood, being the grandchildren of a man who flew the fastest plane in the world that soared over eighty-thousand feet above the earth's atmosphere.

The Momma behind the magic ears, sandwiched between her two babies. Only, mom is no longer the tallest and it seems like the kids sprouted overnight.

Siblings can experience a love/hate relationship. Luckily, there's more love than the latter. Having a sibling who knows what it's like to be hard of hearing provides a unique bond.

Always attempting to reach for higher places, Harper has never met a tree she doesn't like to climb.

Harper loves music. When not using a skateboard to drop-in to a skate bowl, Harper finds ways of turning a board into an instrument. Let's just say that skate decks are plentiful around our home and there is rarely a quiet moment.

I hope Battle always has Harper's back like he does here. There are few people who understand what a cochlear implant journey is like more than your sibling. These kids have developed a secret language of sorts and what's more, a deep understanding of what it is like to navigate life with hearing loss.

The daughter and granddaughter of a record-breaking US Air Force jet pilot, Valli and Harper Gideons take life's challenges as opportunities to soar.

Valli is the mother of two thriving teens who were born with hearing loss. With a BA in journalism from Virginia Wesleyan University and a background as a health and wellness director for the YMCA, Valli transitioned her passion for educating others from a family blog into a prolific writing and speaking career.

Her stories and speaking engagements cover topics that include her own survival of cancer, grief, resiliency, special needs parenting, raising kids with hearing loss and military life.

Her work has reached millions on multiple platforms, including Military Spouse Magazine, Today Show Online, Today Parents, Her View From Home, The Mighty, That's Inappropriate, Hearing Like Me, and Ashton Kutcher's, APlus!

With an engaged community of parents and leaders in the field of the deaf and hard of hearing, she is passionate about her role as advocate and champion of children who are deaf or hard of hearing.

When she is not writing or carpooling to and from a sports gym or field, you can find her walking her two rescue pups along a Southern California beach trail. You can follow more of this family's journey here: www.mybattlecall.com.

Harper is a tenacious teenager who has an insatiable love for books and creating. Despite being born with hearing loss, she hasn't let being hard of hearing limit her from reaching for the stars. When she's not in her workshop building skate ramps or producing her latest YouTube video, you can usually find her on the basketball court. Affectionately nicknamed, "The Fighter," Harper has been known to wrestle a challenger to the ground for a loose ball and never shies away from fierce competition, no matter how big or strong her opponent. Harper has big dreams, and writing a book was one of them. You can check out her latest YouTube videos @Harper G.

Priscila Soares is an artist who has hearing loss. She lives in Vallejo, California with her partner, step-daughter and two sons. She wears bilateral Bone Anchored Hearing Systems. Her youngest son who was born deaf, utilizes cochlear implants. The creator of My Lucky Ears, Priscila advocates for people who have hearing loss, sharing their stories through her mixed media work. You can learn more about her art on myluckyears.com.

Here Are Some Key Terms

Audiogram: A chart that graphs the results of a hearing test. The chart intensity levels are listed on one axis and frequencies are listed on the other axis.

Audiologist: A health care professional trained to evaluate hearing loss and related disorders. Audiologists use a variety of tests and procedures to assess hearing and balance function and fit and dispense hearing aids and other assistive devices for hearing loss. They also perform cochlear implant programming (MAPping). Most audiologists have advanced doctorate degrees.

Auditory Brainstem Response (ABR) Test: A test used to assess the hearing of infants and young children or to test the functioning of the hearing nerve. The procedure involves attaching recording disks to the head to record electrical activity from the hearing nerve and the brain stem.

Bone Anchored Hearing Device: A surgically implanted hearing system that transmits sound to the cochlea (inner ear) by vibrating the mastoid bone (the large bone just behind the ear) instead of by amplifying sound directly into the ear. In young children, these devices are typically worn on a head band until their skulls are fully mature.

Cochlear Implant (CI): A device consisting of micro-electrodes that deliver electrical stimuli directly to the auditory nerve when surgically implanted into the cochlea, enabling a person with sensorineural deafness to hear. How it works: A CI is very different from a hearing aid. Hearing aids amplify sounds that a person can detect, whereas a CI bypasses the damaged portions of the ear and directly stimulate the auditory nerve. Signals generated by the implant are sent by way of the auditory nerve to the brain, which recognizes the signal as sound.

Cochlear Implant Programming: The process of programming, also referred to as MAPping, the device by an audiologist who has special expertise in the field of cochlear implants. This is done at regular intervals. During the MAPping process, the stimulation levels of the CI's internal electrode array are adjusted so that the user can hear the wide range of sounds they may be exposed to.

deaf/deafness (lower-case): partially or wholly lacking the sense of hearing.

Deaf (capital letter): Refers to persons who identify themselves as members of a community composed of deaf persons and others who share in their culture.

Ear Molds: The part of the hearing aid that fits inside the ear and is customized to a person's unique ear shape. They are usually made of plastic or silicone and are custom-fit so they sit snugly within the ear canal. They can have small vents to let air through.

ENT: An Ear, Nose, and Throat specialty medical doctor.

Hard of Hearing (HoH): Denotes a mild to severe hearing deficit.

Hearing Aid (HA): A small electronic device that makes some sounds louder so a person with hearing loss can have access to sound. It is worn either in or behind the ear.

It has three basic parts: a microphone, an amplifier, and a speaker. There are two types of HA: analog and digital.

Hearing Loss: Partial or total inability to hear. There are three categories: conductive, sensorineural, and mixed, which is a combination of conductive and sensorineural.

Hearing: Term used to describe a person who has typical hearing (i.e., "My cousin is hearing and my brother is deaf.")

Microtia & Atresia: Congenital conditions affecting the development of the outer part of the ear (the pinna) or the external auditory canal (the ear canal). Atresia is no opening to the canal and microtia is no pinna/auricle on the outside.

Remote Microphones: Devices used to preferentially deliver the wearer/holder's voice directly into a hearing device. There are wireless microphones that utilize Bluetooth technology, personal FM/DM systems, and sound field systems. For children, these are often utilized in a classroom setting.

Sign Languages: Method of communication for people who are deaf in which hand movements, gestures, and facial expressions convey grammatical structure and meaning.

CPSIA information can be obtained
at www.ICGtesting.com
Printed in the USA
LVHW071449030320
648853LV00023B/457

9 781642 379020